QuickFire,
Slow Burning

QuickFire, Slow Burning

Janette Ayachi

First published 2024 by
Liverpool University Press
4 Cambridge Street
Liverpool
L69 7ZU

British Library Cataloguing-in-Publication data
A British Library CIP record is available

ISBN 978-1-80207-477-2 softback

Typeset by lexisbooks.com, Derby
Printed and bound in Poland by Booksfactory.co.uk

To all the fiery lovers for the ruptures & the raptures

'I am drowning, my dear, in seas of fire.'

Virginia Woolf, *To the Lighthouse*

Contents

Fire in Rio

(After the great fire of Latin America's largest museum)

'Everything shines as it vanishes'

Rainer Maria Rilke

The whole museology of a country
iron material   incalculable losses
national suicide   twenty decades
    of indigenous Brazilian   etymology
water trucks   like high solar winds   empty quickly
flames lick   around the window frames
coffins start to crack   their sides & centre
from the heat.   Ancient   Egyptian   mummies
    giggle up through glass display cases
how the rising Fahrenheit tickles   curls its tongue
under teeth   marble busts & fossil skeletons
    lookout   lit up   by neon orange
riots spill   barricades   sweat   tears &
academic war cries   with backs turned
on their country   as if the crowd outside
    was trapped inside   two hundred years.
Archival showcase   twenty million pieces
    wielded down   to silt & char
how many faces will it take   to see hope emerge
from the fire not fear the fabric of all double helix
    if you burn the past   you torch the future
& the future   looked down from the favela
kicking   its thin scuffed legs   over rooftops.
A bold bonfire   on the second day of September
        just days before
hurricane Isaac   set off on its concorde across

the Caribbean gutted towards South America
with its innards   soaked in the diamonds
    of a tropical storm.
Feather headdresses they went up in breath
left no trace   of their materials at all
the museum self-harming just after closing time.
It had been one of those days;
tourists always touching too much   the light
too bright   the magic unsummoned.
Fractals engulfed   save the relics   as sunrise &
sunset meet for the first time
love the hurt away   the burning has stopped
    in Babylon & started in Brazil
reconstruct from ash said the Andean mummies
    from beyond the grave.
Plumes of smoke   thick with pain   the fire
invents a new kind of fire; mucus.
The only thing intact amongst the rubble
    was that metallic warrior rock
everything else   burnt to bone
        debris & disappearance
apart from dogtooth claw kernel of the galaxy
racing   knuckles   against   flames.
If it survived its passage across the atmosphere
of course a common fire won't kill.
There is an inferno in Rio tonight
volcanoes sleep   & you are out there
as infallible & as radiant   as that meteorite
unblinkingly staring   into outer & inner space
as the hearts of those encircled
burn   in   the   background.

Meteorite

'I drink in one intoxicating shot of Rio after another,
how it would be to gulp and slurp all its offerings
down with you, perhaps one day we'll return together!
Like Frida and Tarsila, lured back by the reality of
macaw song and monkey squawks, stalking spiders and
rat-sized roaches, corn kernel amulets sold by women
with acai stained teeth …'

C.F.

It has been a long vacuous summer without you;
    filled with artichokes of architecture,
        asymmetrical & half-requited loves,
an entire cemetery of buried spent sensations.
I miss where we were once,
    a place I cannot quite recapture,
        but photographs capture & spill you more
beautiful in Brazil;

Samba at the water's edge
    your skin the gold no one can steal or disrobe
        like flaxen sand set against the horizon
where favela kids kick footballs at the sun
under caipirinha sundowners
                on Copacabana beach.

All rivers roll through Rio at some point
    around hillside slums jammed
        with dancing helicoidal bodies
where sewage steers to the sea
under wave cycles of poverty;
    drugs & bullets, then an ex-stasis
        of galaxies come nightfall

over the tourist trails that collect
vacant stares & stained coins.

Yet you are already part of the invisible landscape
   lining paint pots on ledges
     imitating fire with colour,
your wrists balanced against an arch
of graffitied concrete as you stretch
   in tight denim hotpants in the humidity
     tempting & more seductive than oxygen.

In the morning you wake as a magician
   who turns bins into drums for children,
     but they are never quite drums,
& the dust is thick,
   almost deafening,
       & it fills their throats as they laugh.

Equations in Paradise

'The promised land is death'

Joan Margarit

On the nights I melt then solidify without you
                egocentric & tantrum-bruised
we are all river-flow & funeral toll – a mini suicide
each time I surrender to the blind dark
snarled with stars
realising that my clones have bigger closets
down into Hell I go
& I have no desire to play with those little Devils
or prop my cushions up against the char
up through the sandy coastline of cerebral
as I look back to find no footsteps
only one sentient being wiped out
from one self-sabotage to the next
            the old crone weaved into shadow
            as strange as the quick tide
& all the while I run for so many miles
until the awakening of the body takes reign
over my capitalist mind   no dreamy Neptune,
no analysis paralysis just the race of sky & sun
beat & ache & shell around spirit
only stopping to look at myself
in butcher shop mirrors
through the gut-stained glass
I fix my necklace or toss my limbs
until the moon grabs me
from the stench of dead meat.

I am desert wind   stag-leap
over urban pulse made for machine-gallop

& speed & these dilatory women who fall & slip
in their own tears
                    drown in puddles of anxiety
to dampen urgency & flame
I do everything to resist them
for the bad-girl Queens
who refuses to go down with the wreckage
who carry power-cables onto their chariots
tornadoes in their prosecco glasses
who spark light from their fingertips
& never cry wolf
or become elucidated
by their bible of dreams.

absent / present
lost / found
there / here

We wonder. If there is anything.
                    To come back to. At all.

There is a point in the clouds
where a peacock & a Chinese dragon kiss
beaks & snouts engulfed by nebulous
fractured thoughts picked from the wet grout
resisting their time to stick.
In the street café   a couple share
mussels & supermarket roses   in front of me
oil in hair   slime in teeth   fingernails fill
disgust leaves me wide-eyed
but what if you were doused in ingredient
would it make me twitch in the draft
& fold out of a slit in the window   or
would I smile   at your lips' inherent sheen
as bright as a solstice bonfire perhaps
or a Cyprus pomegranate

who is to know, all I know is that you are not here
almost two months since the tollbooth closure
of your thighs   & I can't help but be all water.
A friendship that is dear to me   but still sore
in comparison to what we shared before.

I am grateful for the greatest gift
because what is a poet   with just rapture
& not rupture of love, loaded with a paradigm
of residual relationship made with stardust & dirt
where the absence of those full expansive sighs
up to ceiling & sky creates a clumsy barricade of
false joy for me   it is the only message I can hold
up without tilt   no touching
the rope is not an illusion   not even the
eroticism of invisibility now.

Your smell has left everything   it sits in the grains
of wood   unreachable in planks   lost to hoover
or stepped on by waistlines in bars where songs
swallow themselves.
Instead of send, I press delete
& I am suddenly consumed by the amber of car
headlights & an emptiness that makes me see
only the horror in the mist
that lines all roads home
                the untearable & unmendable
life bond between us
there is no justice in capsize.   only lesson
to stand back   or even levitate higher
in order to see   the true phantogram
                    of the human heart
the greatest & most poignant of all love
is one that resides in the imagination.
The subtle dialogue between gain & loss
between what is   & what is not

or perhaps what never was
              or never could be.

                    We wonder. If there is anything.
To come back to. At all.

Lobster

This was the first scene of our Stockbridge reel,
where the sun tempered against our backs
eyes flicked for shop window displays, smiles
of strangers; our vagrant shadows taller than trees.

The street was smudged
with expired parking meters
our circle became the shape of a drain puddle
absorbing through the grid, brimming clumsy
steps as I clutched the tiny hands of my daughters.

We spot something living behind glass,
a trapped lobster tentatively piano playing its
tentacles feeling for the promise of rock pools
& sand   'it's drowning in there'
a homeless woman shouts up from the curb
marking her presence with exclamation marks.

The young fisherman in a white plastic bodysuit
sees our interest as the girls' caw with excitement
prod the glass with their clammy fingers
& he scoops up the meaty weight, its claws
bound shut with rubber bands, lifts it outside.

People are pulled in like kites on a string
reared away from the endless sea,
the homeless hands & the lobsters' knuckles
both twitch out begging under the new crowd.

Bacchante & New Year

(For L.S)

Lying in snow watching wine   bleed
into   the sleet
clotting under gravel   colouring streets' arteries
where   oak   trees
& tower blocks amputate light   from liquid
shadow.
Smiling through a mess
the scent of berries & mint intoxicating
a crushed amphora   spills grape   tannin
 on my tongue
the tambourine moon symbolled   with stars
& refraction.
Soaked to skin then bone   broken glass
now   dangerous
   fallen woke snowflakes   as the jagged
poised   mouth
of the half-bottle blisters   bubbles that seethe
in the milk-amber   frost   on the horizon.
A slow stream   of bloodletting
on white muslin
        meanders down a drain, I rinse myself
of laughter   step over serpentine
sulphur   veins
to reach your door with a second offering
        still stenched & stained.
You laugh with me   blotting out the semantics
& sirens of life   then like the four-armed Vishnu
light me a cigarette;   dry my clothes
fumble with music   reapply lipstick
reach for the corkscrew   hand me a book.

I notice your gloves   in the surging blur
lit by a faux-diamond ring   on the fabric of your
hand.   You with all your crowned royalties
of mind   a certain gunpowder friend
laughing   under   dim   stars
as the open window let in resonating bells
that triggered guests   to kiss
& a sternly-lit castle   threw up its fireworks
          to a slippery sky.
You with your inviting spider-lashed eyes
     clinking a wobbling wine glass against mine
as I faltered   like   a   loose   hem
trying to pretend
that   this   was not   desire.

QuickFire, Slow Burning

Fire is malicious.   It comes quickly
but extracts delight   in burning slowly.
Love is like this. Grief. All that space now left
after the chasms of fire; burning forests, wildfires, bushfires.
The Earth's lungs cough up phlegm
of choked parrots, charred coyotes,
polluted sea, broken hearts.

           Why is empathy essential   & endangered?

In 1666, a year after the Great Plague began,
four days of fire reaped through London's slums,
timber frames tumbled, bakeries on Pudding Lane melted,
people threw furniture into the Thames.
The fiery vermillion pavements swallowed
a squall of rats whole, wiping the vermin spread.

When Notre Dame caught fire
holy candles & burning plates broke land,
roof destroyed & spire collapsed;
the external disk & dharma,
the djinns, lightning striking the pyramids,
the safe blue skies topped with a dynamite red.

Smoke is a signal toxin,
the heat rules a dislocation of longing
because language doesn't stand still,
it   waits   for   no   one.
All coins have been taken from the well,
gamblers diced a fist in the mouth,
one shot of a carbon kiss for a lucky charm
& the flames bring in the wealth
of customized bones
dismantled from the skeleton of politics.

What happens behind the scenes?

Television reflects reality, reality reflects television;
a gold locket on a necklace
carrying two frayed   dead parents by the heads.
Hong Kong roars up with protests,
tear gas blowers,   the subtleties unhinged
teenagers are missing,   the last photograph
                     time spreads her wings.

Unable to take flight again
I place myself in this house of stone
& moonrise, embossed by what is left behind;
city parks that carousel in the limelight, white-
wash emulsion supports the illusion it creates.

          We search inside the screenshot of our hearts.

I join the neighbours who burn Pandemic news
& unsent love letters in their backyards
under a warped   holy ceremony   of stillness.

          Where is our humanitarian magnificence?

I eat the stars, they remain unaltered.
I'm ready to explore more as the internet feeds
images of unimaginable landscapes;
cultures & love sicknesses
coloured by what the crop can carry
beyond the gardens.
All those new smells & bright sounds,
life resuming as an evolved normal,
life tweaking its resumé
after gap years in Pandemonia
instead of Cambodia.

We live in recovery now
after visiting Pandemonium,

but only once we are captured,
                    can we learn to bond.

                              Survival says we smile for the camera.

All other capitals begin to build upon the ash,
sweep the surface, flames still raging beneath.

Trees in Snow & Letting Winter Go

(After Gustave Courbet, 1856–57)

Grit & mud on my tongue
as I inhale your snow scene
thick & heavy it sinks & insulates me.
Bones shackled; ankles anchored
big beech trees smothered in icing
the first cake of an eager new wife.
A root exposed; cavity uncovered
tugged from its grim icy socket
like an ethernet cable unplugged
after no email from an absent husband.
Fossil footprints faded from yesterday
leaves cluster into coral sponges
& looking closely you can make faces
chalky dabbling of paint becomes;
the head of a dog, a laughing snake,
a voodoo mask pouting a perfect O
like making pictures in the clouds.
Your snow is very much like your sea;
precarious enough to drown.

It is mid-March & snowing again here
in the land of ice & fire, volcanoes in my veins,
the bony undress of the cold grips her claws
in affirmation that this has been an eternal winter
– the confused state of snowflakes nerve me
painting can never quite depict it
the fling & thrash of themselves against glass
never knowing how they melt each time,
over & over & over until
       I miss her like I miss the sun.

Quantum Leap

New Year 2021
still reeling from the last full moon
damp fire pits reignite & champagne pops
Mars-like drones sail a light show
across the landscape
& ship horns bellow from the Leith harbour
neighbours & fireworks & blasting foghorns
belly laughs spluttering like a war has ended
then where to sit in the silence
they ask each other with their eyes
& break it with a giggle
as they all slip in the snow
turn to retreat back indoors
on a slow cuckoo-spring
as if something could still fall from the sky

all stick & none stay & the curtains close
households returning a unified gaze
back to box sets as the gunpowder blew itself
                              to an inevitable
                                        death.

Explosion

(August 2020)

In a country that has died continuously
today Beirut takes another hit
from hoarded ammonium nitrate
confiscated from a Russian cargo ship
kept in storage for seven years
at its scenic port in the harbour.

As chemicals react
heat in the Covid sun
first, there is a small bang
followed by a much larger one
a cauliflower floret of smoke rises
not dissimilar to something nuclear
people filmed the fire from a distance
until the explosion exhaled into a quick cloud
& car windows suddenly sucked into themselves
as if the entire sea had been contained in a bubble
it burst chock-full like a balloon across the land
causing even the furthest away to leap
or to dismantle into cover as debris fired
like a rain of bullets punching holes
into any surface it reached
shrapnel in the streets
states of shock
crisis on top of a crisis
three thousand homes snatched
ceilings fell on hospital patients
buildings shook
trucks upturned
flames spread
through warehouses

smoke breached sunset
streets cobbled in danger
balconies release their stand
sound splinters as it moves
to crack open apartments
lockdown blew apart
all are forced to flee
escaping glass
saving beloveds.

On hospital wards in catastrophe & panic
parents pulled out the intravenous drips
of their terminally sick children
a nurse runs backwards & forwards
arms always flowering
a rescue of newborns
out into the city searching
for other life & more help
electricity cut, cables split,
slashing across the pavement.

What is there to return to in the rubble?

Much like life after a shock blast
everything just fell down
as if a gravity belt had been pierced
calling a whole fleet of people
to hobble on foot to hospitals
where piles of corpses toppled at entrances
with make-shift bandages
wailing bloody faces
amongst children
bricks, dust & metals
hurtling forwards in the air
journalists looked for passports
pens, their breath & sturdy shoes

as over a hundred miles away
on the island of Cyprus
locals felt the blitz
some stilled
some were slightly shoved sideways.

What happens when your world collapses?

Through the kasbah dark night
the names of the missing or wounded
are channelled through distant screens
in the background buried limbs
start protruding through rock
as you sleep then cannot sleep
the alive feel lucky to be alive
but where to sprint now
when uninhabitable homes
keep crumbling possessions.
Unluckiest brothers & sisters
there to weep & there to witness
the demise of your country in minutes
as the firefighters & the healers raced over
what had been exposed
                  with little or any warning.

The smoke reached Damascus
as the skeleton of buildings
shot seismic iron rods
& geometric disarray
in still frame
post-eruption
signalling
more grief
& some clear sense
of a disaster worse than war.

Calamity in the capital city of Lebanon;
I send out my condolences
                in healing prayer & song.

One More & Then We Mourn

It's that time of the oath again
when the slow ticking of clocks turns faster,
concrete & cars merge   with school sirens
at traffic lights   all are eager
for the solid score of home comforts,
suicidal city birds disembark
from last night's gutters   their matted wings
in the standstill of fog & fume
pecking one another's wounds
over the feral charm of wheels below.

Today is a perfect day for a burial:
              one more & then we mourn.

Commuters & acerbic parents criss-cross
pavements & no one has anything left to say
for today encompassed in the echo of muddy
mornings & clotted afternoons with songs
in their ears & tapping fingers, they take to nature
trails instead   where music   is always welcome
& sometimes is swallowed as medicine.

Today is a perfect day for a burial:
              one more & then we mourn.

Behind doors, lovers wait, susceptible to tremor
as they fiddle with packaging, unstrap vegetables
with a powdered burst   resplendent in half-life
              & hunger after work,
cursing is kept for those culinary
& unholy hours   under bedsheets
where love itself is unwrapped & probed to spill.

Today is a perfect day for a burial:
　　　　　　　one more & then we mourn.

With children, I am never lonely though they
keep me plugged to familiar streets
that steal my steps over & over so I chase
through the heart of the capital instead
of around the globe where chambers
are clogged with clumsy ghosts,
subterranean ventricles are laced with noise,
veins are steel-blooded,
　　　　　　　everything seems untraversable.

Today is a perfect day for a burial:
　　　　　　　one more & then we mourn.

The synergies & tragedies of a less loveless mineral
penny arcades on Portobello Beach have nothing
on you in this current state of currencies,
kept in your unclean language; sometimes love is
narcotic, sentinel, cruel as it seems in this lamplit
rain-stained-century,　　　I just cannot reach you.

Today is a perfect day for a burial:
　　　　　　　one more & then we mourn.

The Mad Hatter of Heart Matter

(For N.R)

The Ancient Egyptian debacle
preserving a person's viscera in four canopic jars;
stomach   intestines   lungs   & liver,
the heart   is removed & mummified,
placed back into the vault of the chest
like a candle in a moving lantern
holding the flame
        shielded against the cantankerous wind.

The dark transgresses,
an arrow enters & penetrates;
every passion worth having, worth saving,
contains sulphur, waiting & infinite
        vulnerabilities.

Rarely is the heart harmoniously hammered
to another   often bruised,   conquered,
torn apart   & even eaten by a lover.
Yes, let me eat your scalloped heart
now carnal lust rules with its tall merit
& amorous love
        seeps deep
        into the Western consciousness.

Love is not just a literary concert or soul value,
    it is human intrinsicality;
        the body's entire emotional life & soma.

Take my heart, cut it clean out of my ribcage
& lock it in a covenant like the relics of saints.

Where does the heart belong?

All along beating, before it is gutted,
probed gently by a coroner if we are lucky:
pulse back to life,
patch up the break,
do not fear
& let it fester in my chest,
lift it away before it makes more mess!

This venerated martyr, untimely sphinx,
secular enough to hang inside a great tower
a   tongue   inside   the   bell
banging its edges of the tulip shape wall
gilded in bronze alloy & copper
pricked for a tune

                              tell me;
what is the song   of my heart today
as it feels for its own anatomy,
repairs   itself   in   the   quiet
rejuvenates back to boom
by the young girl in San Francisco who finds you
under two etheric wings
{Narcissism & Nabokov}
a fan of your writing has flair fodder fuel enough
to feed you,   stun you,   make you smile,
patches you up solidly with her golden sentences
                & the language of another together?

Intimate sunsets in New Orleans are on the cards
forbidden pairs stretched over the Pacific Ocean
who folds water on maps
to imagine closer crossings
hearts telling the only tales they know
weighed for judgment with a sprig of rosemary
dreaming with only mean-time in between;
only craving, telepathy, true Eros & no memory
cantering each day   into the sun

as if they could actually write their very own story
& invent   their own kind   of zip-line to love.

Earth Is the School of the Gods

(For Hiroshi Sugimoto)

Minimalist Zen seascapes
divided by the horizon line.
Roethke would be proud,
with such a simple gesture
of composition & light
showing ancient man
without the stain of human history
the first time on the planet
this is what you would see, you said,
& now I have watched nature take over myself
call back   her reigns   with charm
& I waited, conceptually,
the same way you did
capturing the lost human
in your photographs of rainforest dioramas
crouching in the museum.
Humans gone; nature goes on.
I traffic in extinction too,
dream of the last beluga whale
searching for its mate & never finding her
but you were safe with your heart
a solitary mare haunting studios
avoiding touch & disenchantment
for stiff liminal worlds
where new worlds were conceived
& you were able to finally get some sleep.

isolated, together

W.S. Graham & St. Ives

The piece already exists. The place already exists.

When I am on the open road like a free spirit
I am on a Journey of Ascension
I feel lighter, I eat less
& I often levitate in my dreams –

when I reach home, friendships fall apart
sever at the seams, zap energy;
maps, flags, corpse-tags & anchors
– the quintessential quest for the essential line

sometimes a place just steals the right combination
    of poets & artists into its hive:
natives with a sense of belonging,
foreigners with their sense of exploration

shavings / shredding / spherical
erosion / eroticism / miracle
she bites her lower lip
as I read out those words

send the link, join the dots
follow the raindrops on the window
who knows what we might choose to toss
overboard instead of into shadow;

think less, live longer –
sculpt, striptease, deconstruct
with therapy, dance, paint,
pioneering new language, whatever it takes

to glaze the creation with impermanence.
Those days with an easel, nights with

hallucinogens, a string of impossible lovers

lightweights are always faster –
papier mâché pulp how do I emboss thee
& what is it that keeps the movement alive?

Maybe the line took Klee for a walk,
the painter on his knees from vertigo,

see, the perfect profiles
& Gauloises puffed pouts of French women
pebbles filed down to elemental forms,
a Svengali of seductions;

the epitome of everything modern, St. Ives,
then as famous as Paris; a post-war utopia
where jazz drowned out the sound of the sea.

Let's rebuild by tearing down some more –
by awakening primitive forces
prehistoric standing stones jig-sawing portals,
our faith in a brave new world.

'So many ideas come from   and inside
a response to form' said Barbara Hepworth,
then she fell asleep in her studio
    with her last cigarette still burning,
        bones ossified to stone by morning.

Window views are claimed by the landscape,
the stars spitting light
cliffs tainted with iron oxide,
everything you see here. is. deceptively. simple.

How to soften a hard-edged abstract?
Marry it to a love for the natural world.
Where does the body fit without the figurative,
        desire negated now
talked down   from the ledge.

For this kind of self-pleasure give me your
        painter's hand
the vital relationship in art
that saline-drips the literature.

On the other hand,
I am an uncontaminated blue sky
open only to kites.

A hubristic self-focus, amplified by flight
& my basic human instinct for belonging,
trying to be better
        the weightiness of try, try, try
            & the airiness of be, be, be
at last, I am not alone
in being as delirious as diamonds.

Give me your painter's hand, it is the Art of
  Everything & Nothing
now, that I have been shown how to love completely
the heart will naturally compass
such allowance from now on

exaltation & ruination
– life's dear ongoing odyssey,
the world's marbled complexities,
burgundy ribbons, loose threads

that moment when traffic loses its panic
                        & just stills.
Maybe married life is high glamour
to boredom to pleasure to abandon
carbon to its core,

wrestle with your loneliness instead,
your bravery, don't be the glass bottles
recycled at dawn in the distant suburbs

or join the languid sureness of couples
who never miss a clue to secrets over tables,
oh, their entire face as receptive as a single eye.

Dip closer, slip into this room,
I have a giant seabird piñata for sale,
do you know about the hidden life of paper,
its fragilities, a tendency to shrink like lust
or expand like an accordion.

Tear me down & build me back up it cries,
its sense of absorbency craves it,

ceaseless seasons
bribe me with the options –

I was twelve years old when I started
hand-picking papers for poetry

those spiral journals,
until I grew terrified of the holes
open puncture wounds dripping down the page

I prefer the weighty papyrus,
grain-flecked gold-lined
& eager to be tongued by my tentative inks.

Lying in bed replaying the dream I had
sleeping so close to the sea,
that particular night in France
listening to the paralyzing waves
& their neutronic whisper
reminded of how things
always come & then go,
the tug & the pull
the creep up then the chase back
as pebbles staple with jetsam from the tide.

I was ready to know what hunger was like
to run on empty
& only feast when the sunset says it's time.

It was some marvel,
dancing under those telegraphs of light.
Was I insufferable, well, the heart goes on
as well as it can until it can't.

Where does the line go –
after it has constructed the poem, left the page,
palmistry of chicaneries: lifeline, flatline,
& inside it is inclined to leave

but my heart does not empty for you,
its slippery language continues
Isolated, together in the words of Sidney himself.

What do you offer me: a harmony of form, colour,
sound & movement to stimulate the imagination,
all working on something difficult but fruitful.

St. Ives on its side with laughter,
this is the secret, it gasps, to perpetually react.
Whatever happened
could not have happened otherwise,

we spend half our lives in our dreams
so we want to know what goes on in there:
haunting & haunted, hauling the herring
from the harbour, the liquids, the metals.

Let's write & reflect each other,
learn the same landscape, perfect our craft
commit ourselves completely to extending limits,
better,   better,   be,   be

like Peter Lanyon, his shaky aviators
gliding over fields of foxgloves & Celtic Sea,

flying without a cord
or shadow
or parachute
but wanting to know the perspective
so he could paint it true
& even as he crashed,
one last telescopic birds-eye view
after years of circling the skies,
rider of the wind full sail,
that fatal nose-dive into the dirt
as it rippled under him like sand dunes
kite tails pinned to a bed
of soon galvanized coffin nails,
        like an eagle riding the thermals
            trying to lasso the moon.

The Night Robert Burns' Skull Went For A Walk

The moon that night
escaped the pages of *Macbeth*
to nestle in the margin of a sky
where birds drummed instead of sang
& the kirkyard clock summoned midnight
                              with a holy gong.

A phrenologist, spiritualist, Victorian scientist,
surgeon & two workmen swaddled together
to exhume the body of Robert Burns
& raise him from the long dead.
A dank black stone
      of the muddy underworld
      coughed out his skeleton
as the lantern wobbled & ladder shook.
In one fell swoop they dismembered his head,
      40 years after his death
      all that was left was dust
where flesh once slept & accepted kisses,
the heart dissolved & gone living on elsewhere
like Bruce whose silver-wrapped aortic chambers
were tossed into the melee of battle immortalised.
      The heroic spleen & eyeball bereft
       no gore like before
each organ a delicacy, fat for the worm's sword,
      just rot & parched bones now
      aching to be used as weapons.
From the pauper's grave to the mausoleum
with pillars & marble figures
erected at The Plough
      his wife now buried too,

violent admiration is akin to love after all.
They fumbled away from tomb
        towards the plasterer's shop
        on Queensberry Street
swinging the skull in a linen sack,
the light carrying the creak of the casket,
        fondled mandible.
Each man tried their hat on the thing in turn
like the fairy-tale glass-ossified slipper
        "who will be the fairest fit
on this enlarged occipital lobe which shows
his love for animals & children"
        said the phrenologist
& the scientist kept the Paris cast
        for behind glass
of an always-lit university corridor,
the spiritualist held a séance, spoke in tongues,
the plasterer waved, heaved & whistled,
& the workmen
shared a cheese & apple sandwich.
But Burns' hollow orbital sockets
        were as fierce as Fingal's Cave
watching back in amusement,
his spine patiently waiting
through the nocturne
humming a tune
for its reunion.

Disturbing Graves

After four centuries of rule in the Hebrides
the Norse graves secure seats erect as candles
    altar-centre boat burials in Canna aligned
towards home
    when tampered for artefacts
        cyclones rustle horizons
a sierra of skies have faced famine
not drought here, guttural echoes reap across
        the multi-stemmed land
& thunder darkens a diaspora of windows,
with so much visibility the clouds are slashed open
    lightning roots its way
        to the seabed's abyssal plains
like dangling intestines.
    Gabbro, basalt & serpentine
stir in the Earth's basin & the Gaelic water deities
    Burlesque in jetsam shield themselves
from the gore of summer squalls for they know
that storms summoned from disturbing graves
    tend to tomb-pollen wounds
with the medicinal swabs of the moon
& how the birds arrive in the lull
    pecking at the bevelled ground
for their tossed-up offerings
    like forensics working a crime scene
or Valkyries pointing their fingers at the slain.

From Whistles to Screams

'bring home our dead'

Telegram from Achill, 1937

Ten young men camped down for the night
hands cracked & sodden with soil
      they whistle as they wash
sleeves rolled back with precision
morsels of bread passed in a circle;
eyes lowered for their closing communion.
Hay, hammocks & a cobwebbed moon
they dream of their families back home
holidays spent making money in a foreign land
to stock up cupboards for cruel coming winters.
Across the road, my Papa prepared for sleep,
as his father washed & kissed him sweet dreams.
He played his summers with the potato-pickers
      & lay awake at night listening to them sing.
That evening from his window he watched
      the flames feast on the Bothy roof
a blur of men raced to the padlocked prophecy;
they were locked in & no harvest could fill
      the fires stomach.
Smoke choked their spirited whistles
      to soot-soaked screams
the charcoal moon bowed its head in prayer.

The Fire Brigade stuck out its hose reel like a tongue.
Shillings & bones rattled on the railroad back to Achill.

The Anatomy of Memory

    Enlightenment Edina
a seabed of medicine & anatomy
foregrounding the horror
of body snatching
    & some corners still
hold echo from riots in revolt
the crash of shattered
      apothecary jars
& from the Firth of Forth
a whale caved by museum glass
its lulled skull prehistoric
      looming
this is how we learn
the nature of science
            every doctor a white male
every Munro as stern as   the blue whale's
                 vertebrae

1702:
first public dissection in Edinburgh
    a man hung for incest
his fate scheduled
    eight days of dissections

1752:
a man murdered for murder
      the law's thick tongue
granted him to be used
    for anatomical dissection

1759:
the first anatomical study
of

a
woman

I envision, in historical playback,
a doctor riding a sedan chair
    as a locked carriage
through the New Town
tending to women in labour
    & cocooned away
from rogues & thieves
    the cobbled streets here
often beckoned trouble
& behind closed doors
    anatomy uncovered
those first dissected bodies;
    executed prisoners
or taken from hospitals
or out of their graves
or wiped out in private
bodies from the crypt
from the unclaimed dead
not just some body
but somebody
abandoned children
    or foundlings
bound in tincture of saffron
    spell against spell
the demand for fresh flesh
outstripped the official supply
so grave robbers got to work
grim & greedy resurrectionists
with dirt under their nails
jewelled by the recently dead
    a nasty lifting
from porous post-mortem

an escape of the body
from coffins kept
inside cast-iron shells
bondage of chain
around the rim
to protect the dead from flight
graveyards where relatives were found
watching over through the night
teary eyes like governed torches
the ghosts sitting on shoulders
as the hunger reached further
far from cities
    & anatomy schools
       the collapsed human
          was not safe at all
from being resurfaced
to be concealed in cupboards
shielded from the police
the snatched silhouette
their criminal colour
waited through the bruise.
Our Plutonian Burke & Hare
bourgeois serial killers
       spun in the name
of medicine & gluttony
they first killed Mary Doherty
under a storm one night
then Mary Patterson
& so on & on so yes
       let's say a prayer
uncurl our heavy whispers
our Hail Marys
our mother's recipes
because as morning breaches
Robert Knox's anatomy room

leaked as still
as submersion itself
a jetsam serenade of tools;
amputation saws
cranial instruments
lobotomy knives
skull forceps
lined up
like beach paraphernalia
medical laymen
fuelled by murder
& later in the Old Town
the nephews were wearing
the trousers that once
belonged to the dead
oh darlings
not worth a farthing alive
but once knocked
on the head
& carried
to a basement anatomist
they became
treasure-worth
& weighty
mythos of immortality
an expensive cut of meat
don't believe or trust
strangers or body snatchers
who brought
a dozen stale & stiff bodies
to freeze in time's corridor
    who murdered for profit
& wiped their brow
with grubby rags.

Our duo on trial
    their judgement here
& in the afterlife
one free, one boxed
16 martyrs, 16 murders
Hare confesses
avoids persecution
Burke is hung & dissected
a mass murderer released
without charge
    on the run again
Mechlin lace & floss
dockside ports & canals
a finger slice of bread
& time for few dreams
but one was left
to more carnage
a thin line between caring less
    & becoming careless
silver slit fish skin calling
eyeballs muckled out
    with orbital scooping
an eyewitness to his own crime
life ripped out by Justicia
    blindfold & balance
chopped down for medicine
belt unfastened
    flicked from the hip
in one swipe
let's face it
without practice
on fine-tuned windpipes
what would the students offer
inspiration & investigation
flex   together

like bone & ligament
a body swept away from rot
      to pickle in pieces
prisoner-to-night jars instead
how to hold dust in cabinets
wood carved by Hades' claw
at blood level & water levels
time-immortal
circadian clock spent
so sunshine never reaches
& shadows come to mime
& choreograph across
lamented floors
bodies tossed like cattle
carried downstairs
with a swing
      shoulder bent
like a coward-less crowbar
bodies inflated
  in price by death
    & bile & stench
      can you imagine it
some virus would catch them
soon enough if not the winter
so why not mallet
a blunt-force trauma
    to a donor
that hasn't been signed yet
is it still a hit if it's about to fall
    this human life left
at 21 grams a pound
sounding under scalpel
the surgeon's palpable breath
the squire's sharp bell
& measured deconstruction

scalped down to scaffold.

I too have killed you
just to have kept you
        now you live
in memory jars
I store behind
cold ceramic handles
sometimes sectioned
        on display
depending on
the weather
the company
the heart's siren that day
        so as not to fade
                in potency;
one vial for your lips
to remember your kiss
        one for your brain
to educate my perspective
        even the finger
that pointed the blame
        will hold its place
& your reproductive system
on the top shelf
    that I could never
        biologically wind up
    before clockwork
wound it down
    but what else
can a woman & woman do
a fingerprint & crack
on either side of the glass
it's better this way
        the ghost of you

instead of a visceral presence
all the memories & jars
& the absence of you
    finally allowing
my adrenal flow
& parasympathetic system
to feed the organs
    that still pulse
inside my own body
like a circuit mainframe
& tonight here
    in haunted Edina
the sunset continues to show
its skeletal rays
    like a magic trick
& I am arched
    in the half-light
        wetting the arrow's tip.

before the heart, the arrow

The woman next to me peppers her salmon
like a sorceress adding revenge to a spell,
a fire engine screech makes everyone stop thinking
the street café stills apart from the waiter
who collects bottles oblivious to the noisy charm
of tragedy.

Tourists try something Scottish
red-haired lovers lean tables on their sides to kiss,
I wonder how long I have, poets in pubs folding
down notebooks where time stands upside down
grinning under clocks & I can't stop thinking
about group sex & cigarettes hoping for human
connections.

It is three minutes to midday,
the first drink is quick to strike, the music
is not loud enough, smiles become less frequent
as the refrigerator hums its white noise protesting
the heat, window baskets line balconies,
clouds control the sky.

Let me kick unsuspecting stones into rivers
I could drown & write in bars all day
if anyone would let me,
is there a drop-down from this,
perhaps a loneliness, come morning.

The barman swells his pupils
to understand my face, yellow spores of sunlight
streak in garrulous slices.
I am isolated & it is warm enough for me to
undress, coffee halts at its preordained grind.

My love for you has grown as bitter
as the Lysol at the back of Charlotte Mew's throat.
The cinema steps have lost their crease,
people wait at bus stops sitting down
in their own skulls.

    My life is a reel of moving film now
        instead of a stagnant window,
          & love has been more deceptive
        than a hairdresser's mirror.

    The hot cartoon-petalled cheeks
        of wine drinkers in the hotels
        which call themselves houses
        watching the gloomy dance
        of televised ambulances
        stretch across the screen
        ball-gowned in sirens.

Translating The
Transcendental Mountain

Things are shed when people listen to poetry.
Things are shed when people
peregrinate the mountains.
I will be that woman;
a quiet pioneer equipped
with a middle parting;
side satchel, walking stick,
in tweed, not Gore-Tex,
nor climbing gear or gadgets,
who saves her smelt of tears not for pillows
but to embellish the earth that bellows
to swamp nests of idle birds
alongside   the   flood.

I have been that woman;
walking circles from the cliff's girth,
palm against a precipice of granite
given as a new gift from God.
Shrines in the summer rain, fertile
&   full   each   season
with mountaineers who claimed
to own the mountain by mounting it.
The men take to it like athletic swimmers
doing   laps   across
the blunt pyramidal landscape
up the boulder staircases
& never getting lost in the squall beyond the chase
by making it somehow measured;
its nebulous paths, pink feldspar,
a spell of proper pinnacles.

I have been the woman who listened
to the stream in surround sound,
stereoscopically dumbfounded,
until she no longer heard her own heart pulse
where squirrels traced the scaffold of trees
like circus acrobats,
like the practised mountaineer.

What can we resuscitate, in love, in nature;
sprig of heather, needlepoint stars, crystals of ice,
facing that inaudible glare of life
sleeping on the hill & waking to find a blackbird
trapeze-walk your leg,
the mountain opening its curtains
to   a   stage   of   bodies
found on their hands & knees in the drift.
Its dangers must excite us,
to greet a mountain that knew
how to get away with murder –
& what a comfort, to see the world upside down,
like the time I was swimming once
in the waterfall at Glen Nevis,
sometimes I wanted to jump in
from the highest surface
above all the pedalboard structures
regulars hounded beneath
& once I wanted to push my lover in
hoping they would see the fun in it.
What if they might not surface back,
battle the deeper waters instead...
I would make sure no one saw
& tell everyone he jumped
in a terrain with only the stars as witnesses.

I remember expeditions; gunmetal haar,
those same verdigris waters

that tingle the throat if you sip them,
how the mountains are sometimes monsters
from   a   distance
metamorphosed by the dark,
a frantic jutting dramatic head,
grotesque in a helmet of hot weather.
What was beyond the living mountain then;
a funnel into the body's marrow,
a tunnel into tomorrow & back & back & back
a perfect mating ground for soul & soil,
practised for when we return
our borrowed bones to it.

A mountain that mopped the cerebral
soaking up any residue of reality
into something utopian,
a slide into the fantasy of a world
surrendered   to   self
where your book lies holy now in bothies
passed around hillwalkers in communion.
Wallpaper   of   Aurora   Borealis,
mugwort branches, wartime blackouts
why didn't you get bored out there –
because   it   was   exhilarating
to dump the dishes, docile domestic cities
&   all   domesticities
face mother nature in her true divine unravel
each starling-stamped sunrise
when boys made racecourses
competed with climbs & flags over it
we, women, open the mouth of it
& inspect the roots & molars
we peer inside its valleys, its belly
like an ultra-scan, sit up straight
with a stethoscope in hand

to hear its countless heartbeats.
Nan Shepherd lifted its life like a surgeon,
traced great cataracts created by old age & erosion
looking in as it looked back
with a summoning iris,
lenticular against sleet & blueberry mist.

I also need to be alone more than with the tribe,
a talking companion
does quite disgust the mountain,
any overheard gossip & it did not speak.
What a view of the world
from the inside of a cloud
where men disappear except for their whistles
the mountain grows trap doors
& swallows them whole
where sunshine vanishes
like a light-fitted switch that turns off in a room.
I have toppled at the supposed standing
waited to undress to bare my breasts as Atlantis
serenading the Sargasso seaweed,
lifted them out for it to suckle in the din,
in the muck & ichor & mountain dew meeting
in the calciferous cauldron of a cloud
as the ridge gorged its mouth on nipples
we felt full as it fed.
It's not that she was not afraid out there alone
the roar of stags & splash of forests are fearsome
not long after the quiver of midnight,
images & noises leap out of alternate worlds
like lit tulips with mouths agape
for the tale-telling moon.
A song for all the senses, the elementals,
each one tagged with terror;
monstrous rocks, ghostly fog,

the flavours of the berries
for which the tongue cannot repay.

Something about the Scots, they enjoy
the toil & graft of a gruelling lunar landscape,
& welcome the annihilation
caused by wild swimming
for that second after when life floods back
up the violent viaduct into the bone-cup body
from the bottle of infinity
hereunder a hark of bonsai pines
& duck-egg blue whaleback grooves
that breach the sky like an x-ray of my teeth today
roots & rhizomes running like ravines,
snow-capped molars & caves from canines.
Each tooth has three roots, these recesses;
talismanic, limbic
often a sexy nervous simulacrum arises
from the spectacular panorama & chasms.

Nan, arm in arm with the mountain,
not interested in the summit
but in the effect it has on her,
trysting with the beast,
helping her dig deeper into the mystery,
this pilgrimage of life's peaks & plateaus;
joys & woes,
        Nan's transcendental mountain
is where all wild women
when in nature must look to feel & flow.

Jardin Royal, Toulouse, 28th March

(For A.C)

'Here are fruits, flowers, leaves and branches, and here is
my heart which beats only for you.'

Paul Verlaine

To be with you here
    is to breathe amongst the stars
        blossoms flow inside.

Japanese Garden
    holographic pigeons
        blue eyes twin the sky

as the bonsai tree
    steals light from centuries past
        echoes her heartbeat

this day she was born
    there will always be lovers
        celebrating years.

Kill Your Darlings

It has been an easy journal this year
   not much emptying
    maybe the brain fog
is decapitating thoughts
maybe love borrows time
sates the soul, comatoses the search,
domesticity has settled my nervosities
but there is still an underworld yearning
    desire dampens & sparks again
doused in the heavy barbiturates of love
    ash hush of a crematorium
sleepy routines of relaxing together
steps in sync, suspicion discarded,
    a guttural synapse arises
        Earth's dark door unhinges
living under a sky
built of the same things
that keeps our bones in place.
What is this cytology of relationship
seemingly conjoined
fish skin swiped backwards
less elastic, sharp like linen
the fabric of freedom
shredded down to something pocket-sized
    compatible, foldable & clean
        rocked soft by emotional storms?

I had wanted this
   one like no other
    & without any other
the beauty & balance of duality
a furnace to store my love

as it flares over the years
& four decades down
    my body found
its maximum axis of pleasure.
My ink is warm, I am seen
all healing resides in touch
    & the animal cries
our female lungs reserved
for the labour of birth
    & the news of death
& in between our brains swirl
    its forum of chemicals
    like mouthwash
rinsing the palate
of any strange & acrid flavours.
How can you write a good poem
    without murdering your darlings?

El Temblor

A tectonic shift in Northern Peru – a tremor
reached us & woke us out of sleep,
as if we were knocked by a phantom,
two incubi sitting on our backs.

We were rocked from the centre of ourselves,
a seismic rumble that turned us inside out,
grabbed our wombs & merged our bones with
the rods of the building all in a few seconds.

With weak legs I walked to the bathroom,
feeling different, maybe hardly human anymore
but bound to the ground
& somehow made of magma.

Medellín

'We need poetry because the edges are filled with
darkness'

Fernando Rendon

Awakened by gunshots at 2 am
    a rattle through our open window
        the city sucking in its stomach
            as bullets with butterfly wings find
                their designated place to land
            & surround sound opens up
        the space between my ears
    where the heart
sometimes finds itself
                    listening for echo & fire.

Acknowledgements

All my fiercest gratitude goes to my editor, Deryn Rees-Jones, for her insight, vision and patience. It has been such a privilege working together on two books now and my poetry would not have sailed into the world so neatly crafted had it not been for her input. This book would not be a book without all the efforts of Pavilion, especially Alison Welsby, whose virtual presence and answers to all my questions about printing dimensions and such served as a catalyst for the words on the page to align with my vision.

I would also like to thank Creative Scotland for a lottery-funded grant to fly to Colombia for my first international poetry festival in July 2023, to all the organizers at the Medellin Poetry Festival and my translator Valeria B., who read some of these poems in Spanish for me there – my affinity with South America runs deeply rooted.

So much thanks to Alanna, whose force and talent assisted in design and hearing me read the poems over and over until they felt perfect, who helped at every hurdle of writing. Thanks also to my mother, artist and storyteller, Bridget McNeill, who has always cheered my life as a poet and to my two teenage daughters, Aria and Lyra, who are my truest loves and my biggest fans. Gratitude to John McCullough for kindness and sponsorship and to all my friends for the holding, especially to my artist friends Anneli Holmström, Caroline Fulton and Emma Snellgrove, for inspiration and collaboration.

I could not have geared through this phase of my career without all the support above and I feel so much love in my heart and fire at the tail of my spine for you all.

Acknowledgements to the places some of these poems have

first appeared in print: *Scottish Poets*, Vakrxikon Athens, with Greek translations, 2020; *Writers' Shift* anthology, Fruitmarket Gallery, 2022; *Poetry Wales*, Spring 2023. 'From Whistles to Screams' was shortlisted for a Lancelot Andrewes Award by C. A. Duffy and was first published in *Journeys Through Fire Anthology*, Southwark Cathedral, London. 'Medellín' first appeared in *Poetry Ireland*.

Thanks to the Fruitmarket Gallery for the 'Writers' Shift' working with archives and to Edinburgh Park for a poet in residence position, both of which encourage writing poetry from art. Love also to the Scottish Poetry Library for their continued support and poetry commissions both on 'Nan Shepherd' and 'Robert Burns' in the collective 'The Trysting Thorns', who gained quite a bit of media coverage speaking up for Burns' women in 2023!

Finally, a huge thanks to the festivals and organizations who invited me to perform some of these poems and filter them into sound first, a type of editing process in itself, wholly invaluable and lots of fun! Thank you Queer Theory, Neu Reekie, Edinburgh International Book Festival, Cheltenham Literature Festival, The Loud Poets, The Borders Book Festival, Hidden Door Festival, Scotland House on Victoria Embankment, StAnza, and BBC Scotland to name a few.